ALBERTO
DEL RIO

BY NICK GORDON

BELLWETHER MEDIA · MINNEAPOLIS, MN

Are you ready to take it to the extreme?
Torque books thrust you into the action-packed world
of sports, vehicles, mystery, and adventure. These books
may include dirt, smoke, fire, and dangerous stunts.
WARNING: read at your own risk.

Library of Congress Cataloging-in-Publication Data

Gordon, Nick.
 Alberto Del Rio / by Nick Gordon.
     p. cm. -- (Torque: pro wrestling champions)
 Includes bibliographical references and index.
 Summary: "Engaging images accompany information about Alberto Del Rio. The combination of
high-interest subject matter and light text is intended for students in grades 3 through 7"--Provided by
publisher.
 ISBN 978-1-60014-782-1 (hardcover : alk. paper)
 1. Rio, Alberto del, 1977---Juvenile literature. 2. Wrestlers--Mexico--Biography--Juvenile literature. I.
Title.
 GV1196.R55G67 2013
 796.812092--dc23   2011053014

This edition first published in 2013 by Bellwether Media, Inc.

Printed in the United States of America, North Mankato, MN.

A special thanks to Devin Chen, John Smolek, and David Seto for contributing images.

CONTENTS

LAST MAN STANDING 4

WHO IS
ALBERTO DEL RIO? 8

BECOMING A CHAMPION... 14

GLOSSARY 22

TO LEARN MORE 23

INDEX 24

WARNING!

The wrestling moves used in this book are performed
by professionals. Do not attempt to reenact any
of the moves performed in this book.

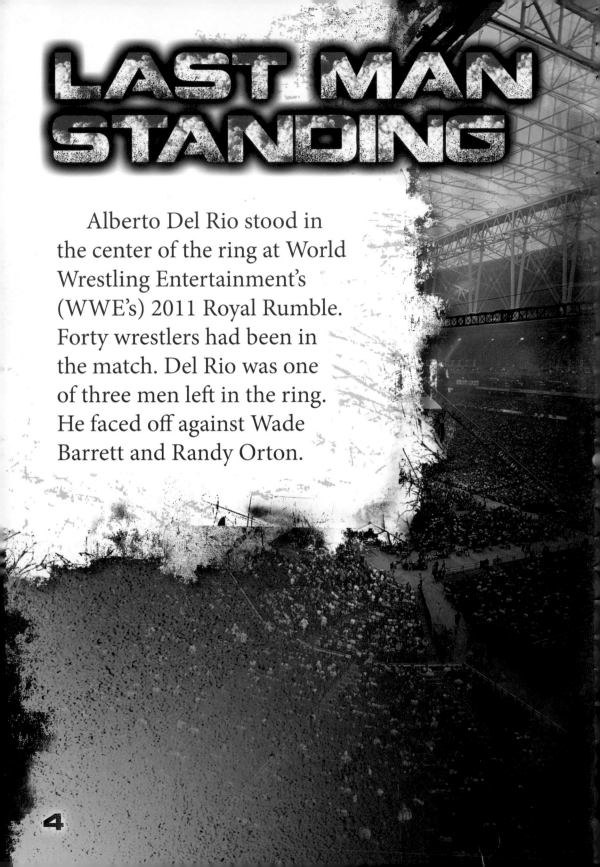

LAST MAN STANDING

Alberto Del Rio stood in the center of the ring at World Wrestling Entertainment's (WWE's) 2011 Royal Rumble. Forty wrestlers had been in the match. Del Rio was one of three men left in the ring. He faced off against Wade Barrett and Randy Orton.

QUICK HIT!

Del Rio's nicknames include The Mexican Aristocrat and The Essence of Excellence.

VITAL STATS

Wrestling Name: _____ Alberto Del Rio

Real Name: _____ Alberto Rodríguez

Height: _____ 6 feet, 5 inches (2 meters)

Weight: _____ 239 pounds (108 kilograms)

Started Wrestling: _____ 2000

Finishing Move: _____ Cross Armbreaker

Orton threw Barrett out of the ring. Then Del Rio threw Orton over the top rope and celebrated. He thought the match was over. However, Santino Marella had been hiding under the ring. He had never been eliminated. Santino attacked, but Del Rio **reversed** the move. Santino went flying over the top rope. The match was finally over. Del Rio was the winner!

WHO IS ALBERTO DEL RIO?

Alberto Rodríguez was born in San Luis Potosí, Mexico on May 25, 1977. He came from a family of successful wrestlers. His father José was the Mexican wrestling legend Dos Caras. Two of his uncles and a cousin were also professional wrestlers.

QUICK HIT!

Dos Caras is Spanish for "Two Faces." José Rodríguez got the name from the mask he wore in the ring. It had a two-headed eagle on it.

Alberto studied **architecture** at Universidad Autónoma de San Luis Potosí. He also trained in **Greco-Roman wrestling**. He eventually earned a spot on Mexico's national Greco-Roman wrestling team.

Alberto prepared to wrestle for Mexico in the 2000 Olympics. However, Mexico did not send its team. Alberto decided to enter professional wrestling. He wrestled as Dos Caras Jr. in both Mexico and Japan. He was the heavyweight champion in one league for more than a year.

QUICK HIT!

Alberto has also fought in mixed martial arts leagues in Mexico and Japan.

BECOMING A CHAMPION

In 2009, Alberto came to the United States to join WWE. He took the name Alberto Del Rio in June 2010. He was a **heel**. Del Rio claimed to be from a rich Mexican family. He bragged about his bravery and intelligence. He started a **feud** with Rey Mysterio.

QUICK HIT!

Del Rio has wrestled in other leagues as Alberto Banderas, Dorado, and El Dorado.

In July 2011, Del Rio won a Money in the Bank **ladder match**. He later used the briefcase he won to challenge CM Punk for the WWE Championship. CM Punk had just defended the title in a match against John Cena. It had been a long, tough match. Del Rio pinned a tired CM Punk and became the new WWE Champion.

QUICK HIT!

Del Rio's victory against CM Punk made him the first Mexican-born WWE Champion.

ENZUIGIRI

Del Rio uses his **signature moves** to wear down opponents. For the Double-Knee Armbreaker, he grabs his opponent's arm. Then he jumps, pulls the opponent down with him, and slams both knees into the outstretched arm. Del Rio charges at his opponent to perform the Enzuigiri. He jumps and uses one foot to steady himself. He delivers a blow to the back of the opponent's head with his other foot.

Del Rio's **finishing move** is the Cross Armbreaker. He performs this move once his opponent is bent over. He grabs the opponent's wrist and steps one foot over the arm. Then he jumps and twists to the ground while still holding the wrist. The wrist bends and the opponent is forced backward into the mat. The Cross Armbreaker is a powerful **submission hold** that has helped Del Rio carry on his family's wrestling legacy.

CROSS ARMBREAKER

GLOSSARY

architecture—the study of buildings and their construction

feud—a long-lasting conflict between two people or teams

finishing move—a wrestling move meant to finish off an opponent so that he can be pinned

Greco-Roman wrestling—a style of competitive wrestling in which wrestlers are forbidden to use holds below the waist

heel—a wrestler seen by fans as a villain

ladder match—a wrestling match in which a ladder is placed in the middle of the ring; the first wrestler to reach the belt or briefcase at the top wins the match.

reversed—turned the opponent's attack against him

signature moves—moves that a wrestler is famous for performing

submission hold—a wrestling move that puts an opponent in great pain or risk of injury; submission holds usually cause the opponent to give up.

TO LEARN MORE

AT THE LIBRARY

Black, Jake. *The Ultimate Guide to WWE*. New York, N.Y.: Grosset & Dunlap, 2010.

Kaelberer, Angie Peterson. *Cool Pro Wrestling Facts*. Mankato, Minn.: Capstone Press, 2011.

Stone, Adam. *CM Punk*. Minneapolis, Minn.: Bellwether Media, 2012.

ON THE WEB

Learning more about Alberto Del Rio is as easy as 1, 2, 3.

1. Go to www.factsurfer.com.

2. Enter "Alberto Del Rio" into the search box.

3. Click the "Surf" button and you will see a list of related Web sites.

With factsurfer.com, finding more information is just a click away.

INDEX

Alberto Banderas, 15

architecture, 10

Barrett, Wade, 4, 7

Cena, John, 16

CM Punk, 16, 17

Cross Armbreaker, 7, 20, 21

Dorado, 15

Dos Caras, 8, 9

Dos Caras Jr., 12

Double-Knee Armbreaker, 18

El Dorado, 15

Enzuigiri, 18

feud, 14

finishing move, 7, 20

Greco-Roman wrestling, 10

heel, 14

Japan, 12, 13

ladder match, 16

Marella, Santino, 7

Mexico, 8, 10, 12, 13

mixed martial arts, 13

Money in the Bank, 16

Orton, Randy, 4, 7

Rey Mysterio, 14

Rodríguez, José, 8, 9

Royal Rumble, 4

San Luis Potosí, Mexico, 8

signature moves, 18

submission hold, 20

The Essence of Excellence, 6

The Mexican Aristocrat, 6

Universidad Autónoma de
    San Luis Potosí, 10

World Wrestling Entertainment
    (WWE), 4, 14, 16, 17

WWE Champion, 16, 17

WWE Championship, 16